VOTES THAT CHANGED AMERICA

Understanding the Role of the Second Continental Congress

History Grade 4 | Children's American Revolution History

BABY PROFESSOR
EDUCATION KIDS

First Edition, 2020

Published in the United States by Speedy Publishing LLC, 40 E Main Street, Newark, Delaware 19711 USA.

© 2020 Baby Professor Books, an imprint of Speedy Publishing LLC

Baby Professor Books are available at special discounts when purchased in bulk for industrial and sales-promotional use. For details contact our Special Sales Team at Speedy Publishing LLC, 40 E Main Street, Newark, Delaware 19711 USA. Telephone (888) 248-4521 Fax: (210) 519-4043.

10 9 8 7 6 * 5 4 3 2 1

Print Edition: 9781541977679
Digital Edition: 9781541977815
Hardcover Edition: 9781541979871

See the world in pictures. Build your knowledge in style.
www.speedypublishing.com

TABLE OF CONTENTS

Events Leading up to the Second Continental Congress 11

Fighting Breaks Out in the Colonies. 23

Two Groups: The Patriots and the Loyalists 31

The Second Continental Congress 39

The Outcome of the Vote 55

The Results of the Second Continental Congress 61

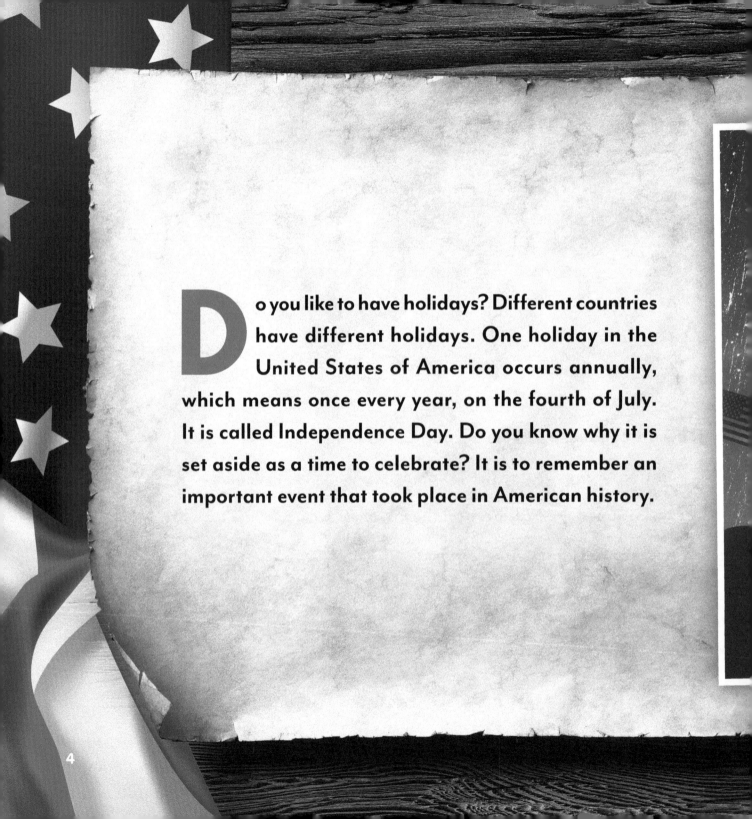

Do you like to have holidays? Different countries have different holidays. One holiday in the United States of America occurs annually, which means once every year, on the fourth of July. It is called Independence Day. Do you know why it is set aside as a time to celebrate? It is to remember an important event that took place in American history.

Fourth of July celebration in the United States.

King George III

At one time, the United States of America was not an independent country. The east coast of North America was made up of thirteen colonies. The colonies were ruled by King George III of Britain. In 1776, the colonists officially declared independence from the British.

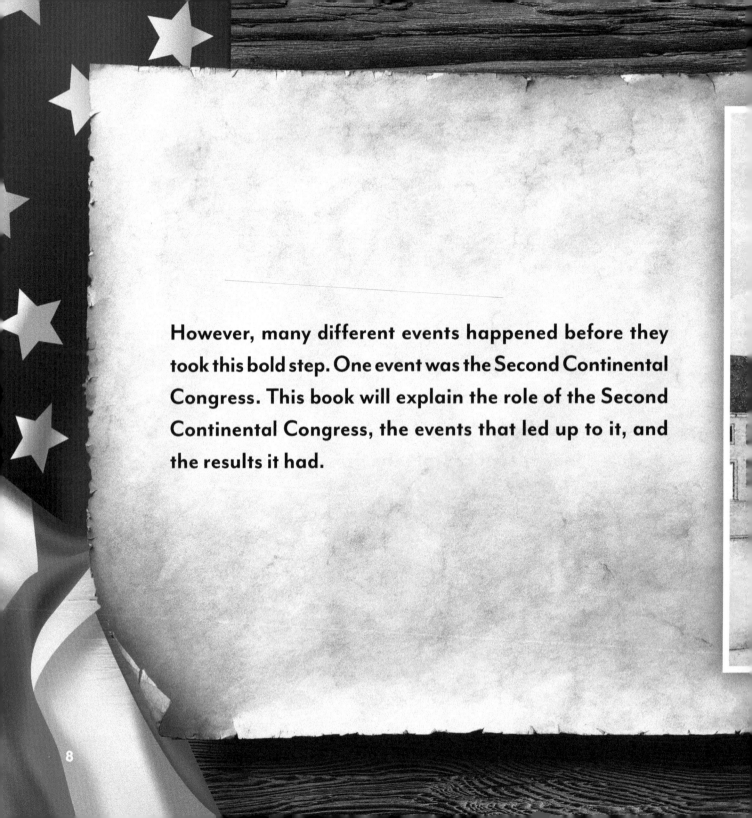

However, many different events happened before they took this bold step. One event was the Second Continental Congress. This book will explain the role of the Second Continental Congress, the events that led up to it, and the results it had.

Independence Hall in Philadelphia where the Continental Congress
met to write the Declaration of Independence 1776.

EVENTS LEADING UP TO THE SECOND CONTINENTAL CONGRESS

Until the 1760s, many colonists were content to live their lives in a colony that was ruled by a king across the Atlantic Ocean. There were local leaders in the colonies who were able to manage affairs. However, in the mid 1700s, that started to change. Britain had debts to pay from The French and Indian War against France for control of the North American continent. To make money, taxes were imposed on the colonies.

Bostonians reading news of the Stamp Act in August in 1765.

American colonists denouncing the Stamp Act.

Many colonists complained about the taxes. They felt that they were being treated unfairly. They had to pay taxes to the British government, yet they had nobody from the colonies to represent them in Britain. Besides, the colonists had fought with the British soldiers in the French and Indian War, so they felt that this was enough support. The king agreed to end some of the taxes. However, more taxes were added, and they were even worse!

Again, the people complained, but this time with more anger. Protests and demonstrations happened. The king sent soldiers from Britain to maintain control over the people. A series of terrible events unfolded in which people were either killed or injured by the British soldiers. Even more taxes were imposed on the colonists. There was extreme hostility against the British troops and their government.

THE FOLLY OF ENGLAND AND THE RUIN OF AMERICA

Stamp Act riots at Boston in 1765-66

George Washington, Patrick Henry, and Edmund Pendleton travel to the First Continental Congress at Philadelphia in September 1774.

The colonists had reached a point where they could no longer tolerate the harsh and unfair laws that were forced upon them by the British king and his members of parliament. They decided that they would have a congress, or an official meeting. Representatives from the colonies met in Philadelphia in the early fall of 1774 to discuss what to do about the awful way the king was treating them.

Their meeting was called the First Continental Congress. At the congress, it was decided that a document would be drafted which stated the colonists' rights. It was also agreed that the representatives would notify King George III of their objection to the taxes. The representatives did not want to have to be disloyal to the king, but they wanted him to know how they felt. The representatives agreed to meet a second time the following year if conditions had not improved.

Chaplain Jacob Duche leading the first prayer in the First Continental Congress at Carpenter's Hall, Philadelphia, Pennsylvania, in September 1774.

FIGHTING BREAKS OUT IN THE COLONIES

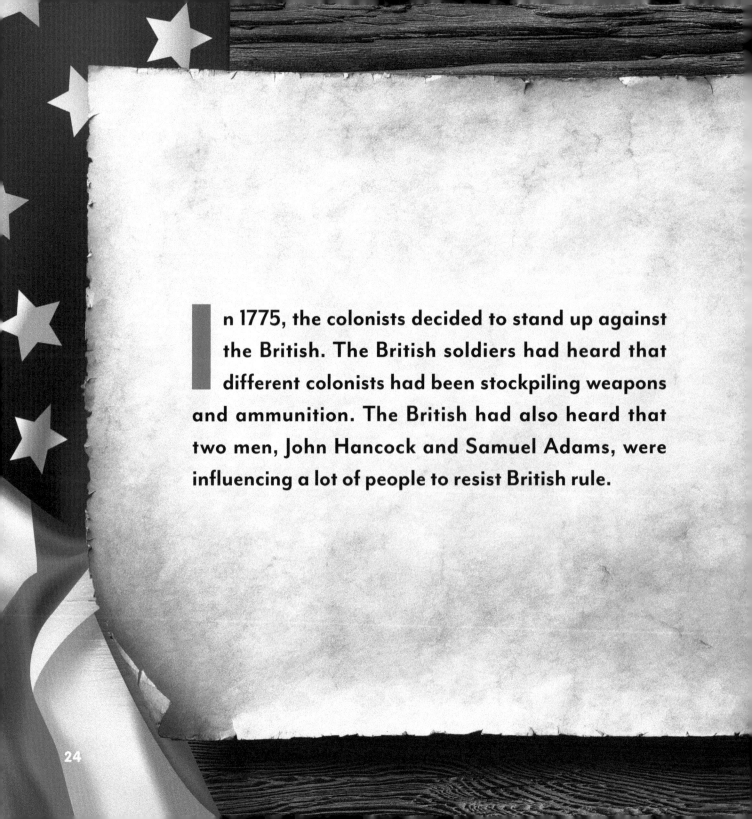

In 1775, the colonists decided to stand up against the British. The British soldiers had heard that different colonists had been stockpiling weapons and ammunition. The British had also heard that two men, John Hancock and Samuel Adams, were influencing a lot of people to resist British rule.

John Hancock

Samuel Adams

One day, the colonists found out that Lexington and Concord, two towns near Boston, were going to be raided by the British soldiers. Along with seizing the hidden weapons and ammunition, the soldiers planned to arrest John Hancock and Samuel Adams. Before the British soldiers could do any of these things, however, the people in Lexington and Concord were warned by three men who rode on horses: Paul Revere, William Dawes and Dr. Sam Prescott. The mission of the British soldiers was thwarted.

William Dawes

Paule Revere

Battle of Lexington, April 19, 1775

Both the British soldiers and the colonists suffered losses. However, the British were shown that the colonists were willing to fight for their freedom and independence. The date was April 19, 1775. It was an indication of what was to come.

TWO GROUPS: THE PATRIOTS AND THE LOYALISTS

The conflict in Lexington and Concord was fresh in everybody's minds. Many people started to fall in one of two categories, being a patriot or being a loyalist. Patriots were people who wanted independence from Britain so that they could exercise the right to self-government. They were strongly against paying taxes to a government and getting nothing for it in return.

They felt that this was extremely unfair, and they wanted the king to see their viewpoint. The patriots felt that the taxes were forms of punishment for disobeying the king's orders. They said that it was as if the king were punishing disobedient children. They started to say the phrase, "No taxation without representation" to show how they felt.

Patriots were people who wanted independence from Britain so that they could exercise the right to self-government.

The Loyalists, on the other hand, did not want to become independent from Britain. Although they disagreed with the taxes just as the patriots did, they had hoped to work out a peaceful agreement with the king. The loyalists also thought that it might be possible for the colonies to return to the same conditions that they had before the heavy taxation.

They were not in favor of fighting a war against Britain. They wished to continue being subjects of the king. Both groups did, however, think that the people in the colonies should enjoy the same rights that the people in England enjoyed.

The Loyalists did not want to become independent from Britain.

Fighting had already started between the colonies and the British.

As time went on, it became obvious that the king was not going to relent. In fact, he was upset at the colonists and thought that they were in the wrong. What is more is that fighting had already started between the colonies and the British. Something had to be done to establish how to move forward.

THE SECOND CONTINENTAL CONGRESS

Once again, representatives met in Philadelphia, Pennsylvania. The meeting was called the Second Continental Congress and since it was May 10, 1775, it was less than a year after the first Continental Congress. It was also after the British had recently marched into Lexington and Concord.

Carpenter's Hall, Philadelphia, Pennsylvania, meeting-place of the First and second Continental Congresses.

Representatives debated on whether the North
American colonies should be free from Britain or not.

The delegates, or representatives, had some tough decisions to make. The most important area about which the representatives debated was whether independence should be declared from Britain in the North American colonies.

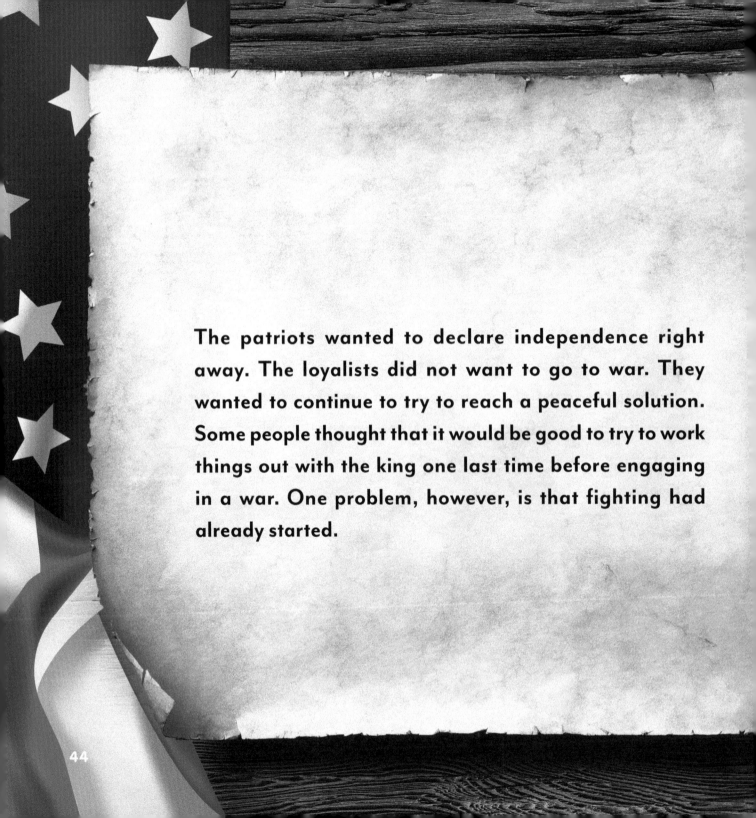

The patriots wanted to declare independence right away. The loyalists did not want to go to war. They wanted to continue to try to reach a peaceful solution. Some people thought that it would be good to try to work things out with the king one last time before engaging in a war. One problem, however, is that fighting had already started.

Committee writing the Declaration of Independence 1776: Franklin,
Jefferson, Livingston, Adams and Sherman (left-right).

The Olive Branch Petition was adopted by the Second Continental Congress on July 5, 1775, in a final attempt to avoid a full-on war between the Thirteen Colonies and Great Britain.

The representatives at the Second Continental Congress continued to discuss options for weeks. They eventually came to an agreement. They would offer King George III an olive branch. Offering an olive branch is just a figure of speech, which means you wish to come to a peaceful arrangement. John Dickinson, along with some others, drafted the *Branch Petition* or the *Olive Branch Petition* that would be sent to King George III. A petition is a document which requests a change or changes to be made.

The British military was the most powerful army that the colonists knew.

The representatives decided that the colonies needed to have their own army. Up to this point, groups of different militias were fighting the British troops. Although the militiamen had gained confidence from having won some conflicts with the British soldiers, an official army would be necessary to engage in a war. The British military was the most powerful army that the colonists knew so they had to make sure they were prepared to go into a war with them.

The name for the new official American military force was The Continental Army. John Adams was the one to suggest it and he also said that it needed to be led by a general.

John Adams

George Washington, who had served in the French and Indian War with the British, was selected to lead the army. Since George Washington had military experience, it was felt that he would be the best choice as the Commander-in-Chief. Washington agreed, on the condition that he not receive any money for doing it!

George Washington is appointed Commander-in-Chief of The Continental Army.

The minutemen, a group of men who had already been training so that they could be called upon at any time to fight the British, would become soldiers in this army.

Minute men of the American Revolution

As for an outright declaration of independence from British rule, the representatives were divided. While many people wanted to declare it right away, others were unsure. In the end, the representatives decided to put the decision to a vote. They would ask the people in their individual colonies to tell them what they wanted: independence or not.

A depiction of the Second Continental Congress voting on the United States Declaration of Independence.

THE OUTCOME OF THE VOTE

An overwhelming majority of the colonists voted in favor of declaring independence from Britain. After the rebellion and conflicts so far, it seemed highly unlikely that a peaceful outcome would happen. They were right. King George III was so upset with the colonists that he did not even read the Branch Petition that was sent to him.

The signing of the Declaration of Independence in Congress, at the
Independence Hall, Philadelphia, Pennsylvania, 4 July 1776.

One thing which helped to sway the vote in favor of a declaration of independence was a pamphlet. It was written by a man named Thomas Paine and it was given the title, *Common Sense*. The pamphlet was written to show the people why it made sense to vote for independence.

Thomas Paine

It questioned why the colonies should be ruled by a monarch, especially one who lived 3000 miles across an ocean. The British government was imposing laws and taxes that were hindering and harming the colonies. Moreover, this is the type of government that the colonists did not want. They could do better on their own.

Title page of the pamphlet, Common Sense, published in 1776.

COMMON SENSE;

ADDRESSED TO THE

INHABITANTS

OF

AMERICA,

On the following interesting

SUBJECTS.

I. Of the Origin and Design of Government in general, with concise Remarks on the English Constitution.

II. Of Monarchy and Hereditary Succession.

III. Thoughts on the present State of American Affairs.

IV. Of the present Ability of America, with some miscellaneous Reflections.

Man knows no Master save creating HEAVEN,
Or those whom choice and common good ordain.
THOMSON.

PHILADELPHIA;
Printed, and Sold, by R. BELL, in Third-Street.
MDCCLXXVI.

THE RESULTS OF THE SECOND CONTINENTAL CONGRESS

The colonists had come to a decision to declare themselves independent of British rule. One of the representatives from Virginia, Richard Henry Lee, spoke up. He told the other representatives that all the colonies had come together.

Richard Henry Lee

As states, they have the right to be free and independent. The representatives went in favor of the vote from the colonists to declare independence from Britain. In other words, they were voting to go to war against the British.

Delegates signing the Declaration of American Independence.

Thomas Jefferson, one of the representatives, was chosen to draft the official document that would be submitted to King George III. The document would be clear and precise. It would let the king know that the people wanted a democratic government.

Thomas Jefferson

Thomas Jefferson reading his rough draft of the Declaration of Independence to Benjamin Franklin in 1776.

This is a government whereby the people elect someone who is running for office. The elected representative will then work for the people and make decisions for them. The people did not want to be ruled by a monarchy, a government which has a king or queen. In short, it would state that the colonists were declaring independence and why they came to this decision. It would inform the king that the colonies considered themselves to be states, free from British rule. The states would form their own government.

The Declaration of Independence received official approval on July 4, 1776. It was sent to the king and the British government. The result was that the war would be official between Britain and the colonies. Although the Revolutionary War would continue, in the end the Continental Army would prove to be victorious over the British military.

Reading the Declaration of Independence to cheering colonists in Philadelphia July 4, 1776.

The Second Continental Congress played an important role in moving forward with independence. The Continental Army and the Declaration of Independence resulted from it. Moreover, the representatives at the congress went to the people to vote on their future. This action showed the type of government that the people would have in the new country of the United States of America, a representative government.

Visit

www.speedypublishing.com

To view and download free content on your
favorite subject and browse our catalog of new
and exciting books for readers of all ages.